Brickfields

my life at Brickfields as a potter, painter, gardener, writer and cook

by Mary Wondrausch

designed by Michael Tighe

Published by Mary Wondrausch OBE

Previous page: This is a terracotta mural. Three of us made it in 1983.
Opposite: The drawing-room door with 'Madame Alfred Carriere' rose.
Overleaf: An old galvanized basket hung with my mother's 19th-century crystal chandelier drops.

contents

introduction

Brickfields, a modest cottage in Surrey that I bought for £3,250 in 1955, maybe now worth a great deal more, has been the somewhat still centre of my wayward life for forty-six years.

It had in the 19th century been a brickyard, although nothing, except the prevalence of red lumps in the earth, remains to establish this. I have photographs of the old brick-yard manager (see page 19), and I believe at one time eleven people lived in the cottage. It is a timber-framed building, the original hovel dating from 1550, the present kitchen being the outshot. I like to think that maybe two oxen rested there 400 years ago. There is an elm tree in the garden, sadly killed by Dutch Elm disease, that is said to be 500 years old. But it is only really now, in the year 2004, that I have come to realise, as a potter whose inspiration comes from the 17th century, that it was meant that I should be here. Here in this magical place full of dragonflies and birds and hogweed.

All potters are particularly of the earth, and because I work in slipware and with a red clay I am exceptionally earthy.

It was only when I moved my workshop from the town to the stable that I began to clothe the house with old textiles, kitchen bygones and 19th-century pots. Before 1984 there had been my children, students, a donkey and bantams, all of whom made my life in those days a fairly 17th-century existence. My workshop, formerly a stable for five working horses, was roofless, with elder and ash rooting between the bargate stone flooring. There was also a quarter-acre of docks and nettles, and rotting sheds fenced by corrugated iron.

Now I store my clay in Emmie the donkey's old stable, my shop is in the old garage and the main structure is where I work/pot. Three years ago the garden was famous and open to the public, but now it is a wild and comfortable place with a grand herb garden and mowed paths leading to the hogweed and to surprising fountains and other installations/'sculptures'. The back of the house faces south-west and retains most of the old features, while the north elevation appears to have been gentrified in the 18th century.

Fortunately for Brickfields I have never had any money, so the structure both inside and out remains modest and unspoilt, although overflowing with old pots and pans. Maybe grass invades a kitchen corner, and a rose the bathroom, logs chip the great bricks in the inglenook and rain dampens the yellow room, but still it is beautiful.

I have riotously painted all the furniture possible, the walls are festooned with my paintings, and chillies and garlic curtain the great kitchen beam.

How rhapsodic this sounds, and to many people it is just that. Nevertheless, living in these 400-year-old walls is demanding.

The garden has changed radically since 1984, when I moved the pottery from Godalming to the reconstructed stable. For the first time in ten years I was around the place all day, full of optimism for my new venture, which would include residential pottery courses. My beloved donkey Emmie, who had mowed the grass for twenty-nine years, was dead. We needed a car park, paths through the rough grass and different corners where we could sit and drink wine and eat marvellous food.

Ultimately the courses became too onerous, there was an increasing demand for my pots, more customers found their way here and I amused myself by making outrageous fountains from found materials. This proved an attraction for visitors and I was persuaded to open the garden to the public.

I wrote a little essay for these occasions (see page 76), when about 300 people would wander in a slightly stunned way around the various incongruous installations. Naturally this entailed having a marvellous gardener and at least two hours a day gardening for me. Articles were published both here and in Japan and the whole project became too demanding.

I was a potter not an entrepreneur. Many journalists came to photograph the house and its interior for various magazines and books and my previously boundless energy began to diminish.

With the onslaught of arthritis I ceased gardening and put all my strength into the pottery and into revising my book *Mary Wondrausch on Slipware*, which had gone out of print. All the black-and-white illustrations were replaced with good colour. This proved a mammoth task, with many museums

Receiving an OBE in 2000 for services to the arts. I am wearing a papier-mâché hat, based on my plates, made by Niki Williams.

being extremely co-operative, as were potters and photographers. I wrote new chapters and made additions, and at last this new impression is in the bookshops.

I enjoy writing and I enjoy food, so for the last six years I have attended the Oxford Symposium of Food and have written various papers on the history of food related to its artifacts.

Over the years I have been researching and assimilating archival material on Dorothy Hartley (*Food in England*) and am, far too slowly, writing her biography.

Her writings were a major influence on my life, and when I first read her book it enabled me to make some sense of the 16th- and 17th-century ways of life that must have continued in my house.

My efforts at making soap were pretty gruesome, home-made furniture polish a disaster. But we cooked pig's head and trotters, I skinned rabbits and made terrines with Elizabeth David's cookbooks propped alongside Hartley.

Bread was baked twice a week, and late summer harvesting is still exhausting with the blackberries and damsons to be jammed, followed by quince, apples and medlars. Then there is the marvellous mushroom time when I go foraging after work each day gathering enough funghi to last me through the winter and as gifts for all the family.

I have always managed to do some painting during my annual French holiday and have had two or three exhibitions and continue to sell painting off my walls.

To a slipware potter, drawing is vital, and each day I do this both for pleasure and as a discipline.

As the house is continually overflowing with books, pots and bygones, I have been forced to think of my poor children who will have to somehow dispose of this mass of material.

During 1996 I made my will, leaving large bequests to various museums and libraries who were agreeable to receiving the material and who were in a position to catalogue my work and give students access to it.

All these different and consuming interests, including my use of the camera, have encouraged me to gather the material together to form this litle book.

the history

Some past history and a story of the recent history and of my creative life in this little house

The history: extract from the Domestic Buildings Research Group survey

Brickfields was built as a small, two-bay, one-and-a-half storey timber-framed cottage with the smaller bay as a framed smoke bay. The date of the building was the end of the 16th century. There is a large gablet for the smoke and an original outshot behind. A fine brick 18th-century house was added in line, and the old house was retained as a back kitchen and scullery.

Brickfields is important because it is a very small early house of a type which has not usually survived.

The cottage is built on the eastern edge of Compton. It is surrounded by meadows, and to the south is one which had been the brickfield. The Georgian house is built of good field bricks which have a surprising variety of sizes. They are a good rich colour.

The appearance of the house is unusual. There is an unusually tall prim house attached, in line, to the low cottage whose timber-framed walls have been replaced in brick. The new house has two outside chimney stacks. The inglenook hearth is at the back, and the smaller parlour hearth is at the west end. Both have stone in the lower part, with galleting. The old cottage is one of the smallest yet found.

The brick house has the central entrance directly into the living room and the large hearth. This was built out at the back because the old house was retained at the side. Through is the parlour. This was panelled. The hearth was in the end. There had been a window beside, but this is now blocked, and the space is turned into display shelves, nicely moulded. Other windows are cased, with shutters and side panels and panels above, all matching. This is an elegant feature.

Opposite: The front of the rather prim main house and the earlier small cottage to the left. Above: Impressions of what this earlier part may have looked like when constructed in the 16th century. Right: This close-up of the south wall shows the wonderfully weathered old brick made on site, and the bargate stone with stone chip galletting in some of the mortar.

Above: The back of the house (when my garden was open to the public), showing the huge chimney, and the little conservatory I built in 1980, with the intention of growing tomatoes (joke). This proved unsuccessful, so we sit here in the winter when the sun is shining.
Opposite: An old photograph from around 1890 with the ladies of the house standing beside the same chimney, and showing the interesting original lattice leaded windows.
Left: The 500-year-old elm tree which finally succumbed to Dutch Elm disease in 1988, with an owl made from an old enamel laundry 'basket' and a painted slop-pail lid.

Above: The kilns at Brickfields were still in use in the 1890s,
but there is no record in the census of brickmakers there after 1906.
Opposite: Mr Allard and his wife, who were the owners at that time.
You can see from the end of the house, visible to the right of the picture,
that it has not changed a great deal since then.

the rooms

Decorating the interior of my little house has been both a passion and a pleasure for some thirty years, with European folk art being my main source of inspiration

My painting of the north window in the blue bedroom with mocha jugs, a Mexican clay house and 19th-century pharmaceutical jars.

I have painted every corner of Brickfields and this is no exception. My painting shows this justifiably well-known view of my kitchen. Everyone loves the row of Brannham earthenware jugs on the window sill. The chillies hang from the 16th-century beam. I got the inspiration from paprika peppers in the Budapest market.

my kitchen

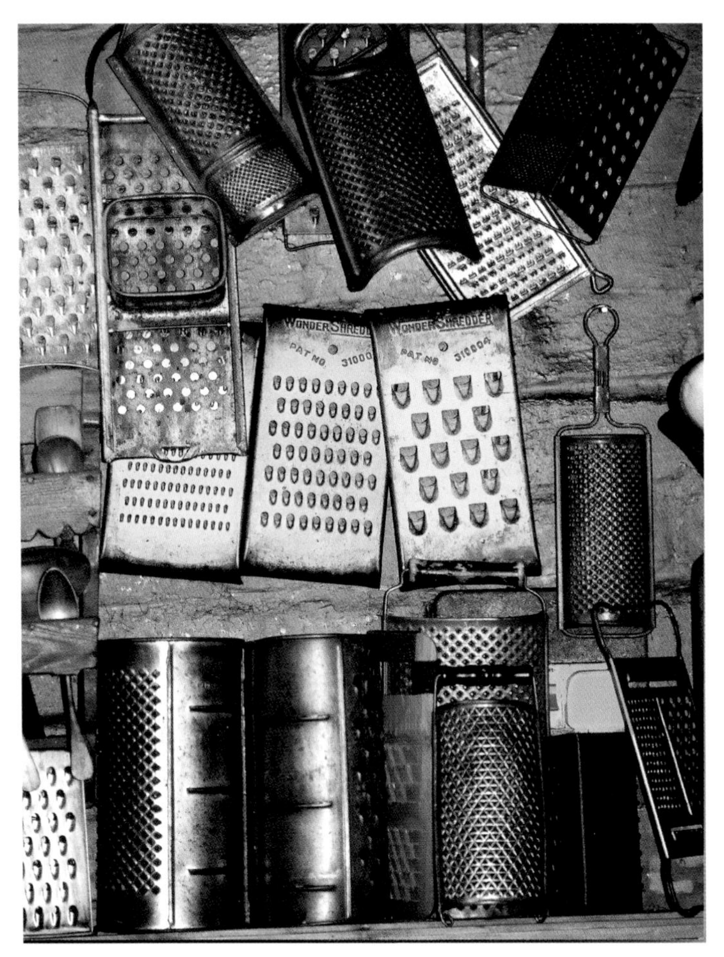

Main picture: A broader view of the kitchen, previously a 1550 outshoot to the hovel. I like to think a pair of oxen once lived here. The ladder-back chairs are 18th century; the one on the right is from the estate of the master potter Henry Hammond.
Opposite, left to right: one of my Christmas cards; foot for the central kitchen table – I threw this as a facsimile of 18th-century potters' work – it keeps the legs dry; cupboard knob, made by me.
This page: part of a collection of elderly kitchen graters; a collection of spoons; this 'chandelier' is an East European game larder, hung with early 20th-century kitchen strainers and whisks.

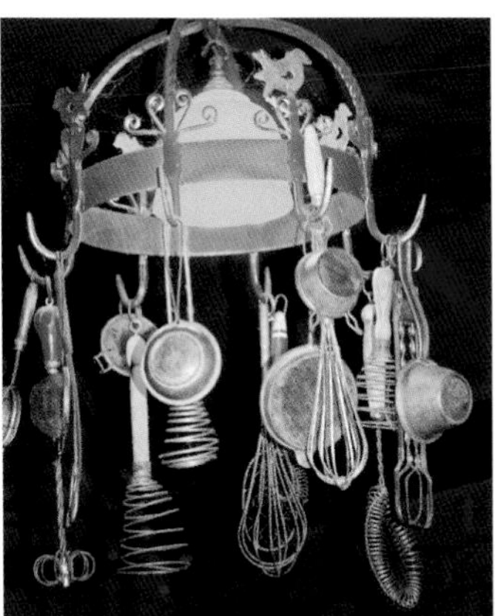

my painting with Tibs and Augusta

Above and opposite, above: A view of the kitchen looking towards the back door. You can see the old coal hods in the photograph and the 17th-century rose-red brick floor. This door leads out to the garden and the pottery. Opposite, below: a row of early polishers, peelers, graters and slicers that sit on the small central kitchen table, and French enamel cafetieres.

Right: I first had the idea of painting the beams in the drawing room after a visit to Bruges in the 1960s. The wheatsheaf design was made with the laid pointed brush (my students helped me). The revealed ceiling between the beams is *sang du boeuf*, an old colour much used on the Continent. This room has always been dark and is not used a great deal in summer. Above: a rough sketch of the corridor between this room and the kitchen.

My painting of the drawing room shows the original inglenook fireplace built around the end of the 17th century. In the winter, this great fire devours oak and larch and beech, giving off a great and comforting heat.

Folk art – ideas from everywhere

Maybe it was in 1980 that the interior of the house was decorated; a difficult job as there are no right angles and lots of wandering pipes.

The kitchen colours were inspired by the canal long boats – I expect by now it is clear how interested I am in folk art. There is not much in England, but some in Wales and Scotland. Our barges are famous for their decoration.

I chose a strong red for the kitchen walls, a dark green for the ceiling and an ultramarine door. Later we stencilled the walls using old oily yellow paper and distemper and pigment. This work was done long before stencilling and paint effects became trendy. The dark walls and ceiling led to the great cross beam and the white ceiling beyond. It was later that chillies emerged to festoon the 16th-century purlin.

I fear the collection of cooking bygones has got out of hand as you can see from the photos. I'm particularly fond of graters (see page 25).

The drawing room has a *sang de boeuf* ceiling, and the beams are painted with ochre wheat heads. The walls are a very strange colour, sort of buff/pink and stencilled. Art students living with me helped here – it was quite a party. Years later when I bought the Irish dresser I painted the

Above: I painted this little table in acrylics for a customer.
Left: A little 1920s cabinet that I embellished with a vase of lilies and carnations.
Opposite: Two of my wall paintings inspired by Swedish folk art.

Previous spread: This marvellous Irish fiddle-fronted dresser in the drawing room, dating from the early 18th century, holds my eclectic collection of European slipware. There are many pieces from Winchcombe, some from Yorkshire and of course the French, German and Hungarian pots that reflect simple rural traditions. They are mostly functional – the strange round porcelain object in the right-hand shelf is a 19th-century meat tenderiser; next to it is a lemon squeezer from the Duke of Devonshire's old kitchen.

Opposite, above: my painting of the north side of the drawing room. In the same view, below, the curtains are made of hemp from Transylvania. The motifs are hand-blocked with indigo. I found them, just as they are, on a linen shelf in the local saleroom fifteen years ago. The little mirror belonged to my mother and is Georgian.
Above: This painting is of my bedroom – the head for beads is by me, next to the wonderful 19th-century Syracuse wine jug. The little display cabinet was made by my grandfather; the bed cover is Gujerat.

wall to link it to the wooden Swedish horses on the window sill – my mother was Swedish; (see page 32).

The great fire burns well and the logs rest on the ashes; the glow sometimes remains all night.

My bedroom takes the colours from ancient Greek rooms – turquoise and terracotta – the ceiling covered (in the French manner) with a Hardy Amis wallpaper, joining the north and south landscapes with a trellis effect.

Charleston was a big inspiration for attacking the furniture: most of the simple pieces take on an unexpected exuberance.

I made the tiles to go over the bath, inspired by our little bantams. Indian and Turkish textiles grace the floor and the sides of the bath. This 9' x 6' room is the upper part of the original 16th-century house and would originally have been reached by a ladder.

The stairs go round a corner to the second floor (pages 40–41), which became my studio and where I slept when the children were little. The walls are hung with Caucasian carpets. There are Turkish

Opposite: I made these bathroom tiles – slip-trailed in the traditional way – with a honey glaze. We used to keep bantams and these represent the various old breeds. Above and right: These plates and the large jug are in a similar style and are part of my everyday stock in the shop.

LA MUERTE DE PICASSO

Previous pages: my studio/spare room at the top of the house – covered in oriental carpets and hung with fishing floats. The chair is early 20th-century American and my painting is of the same subject. The plate is mine.

rugs on the floor and old cork floats (found in a Catalan rubbish tip) droop from the great beams. I put the windows in up here when I bought the house in 1955. Previously there had been only a 4' square entry in the floor. To the builder's dismay, I kept the lath and plaster wall exposed. This divides the studio from 'the tank and junk room'.

On the first floor is the yellow room, with daffodil-coloured walls and sky-blue ceiling. I painted tassels all around the ceiling and painted the new fireplace surround. It is smothered in 19th-century pots from Thun in Switzerland.

Next door is the blue bedroom, with a huge decorated cupboard and old-fashioned sprigged wallpaper (see page 25). There are lots of my paintings on the walls. The bed has a hand-dyed indigo cover and we change this often with unusual textiles, depending on who is visiting.

The whole of the inside of the house is full of objects found on junk forays both here and abroad, and is extremely difficult to dust.

Right and opposite: These jugs all come from the same pottery workshop in Devon and date from the late 19th and early 20th centuries. They were used to store milk and to keep it cool. To me these Brannham jugs are the most beautiful of the many milk pitchers of the same period, made by most country potters throughout England at that time.

Above: This is the original part of the 16th-century hovel, and is now my study. The ceiling is just 5'9" high. The room has a stone flag floor on the earth. The blocked-up 'fireplace' on the right (out of the picture) was without a chimney and leads to a smoke bay. On the windowsill is a row of early 20th-century Wrecclesham owl jugs. The curtains are French.
Right: I designed this large cushion, Joy Huter machine-embroidered it and Anna Crutchley made the cord and tassels.

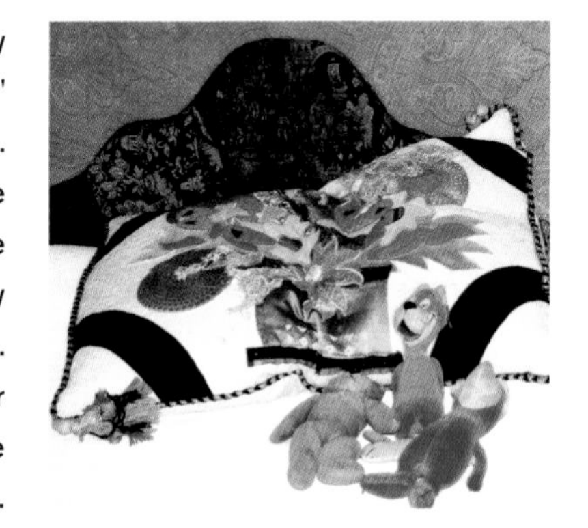

Above and overleaf: I painted the yellow bedroom with a tassel frieze around the top. My son Hugo built this fire surround for me with specially sized shelves to house a collection of elaborate 19th-century Thun ware, and I painted it. (This jug, left, is a very fine example of this Thun slipware from Switzerland). The strange table was painted by a pupil of Augustus John in the 1940s, and the two oval dishes above it are early 20th-century faience from Provence. The curtains are hand-woven and embroidered and under the window is an 18th-century Chinese silk, adapted from a screen.

This page: Early 20th-century Swiss pots in the yellow bedroom.

Opposite: Bright European plates in my downstairs shower-room– mostly seen by men!

PAPER
750
HARRODS

the food

I love food – growing, cooking, eating and writing about it.
Also drinking the wine that makes every meal a celebration.

Opposite: *The Mexican Candelabra*, my gouache painting of 2004.

My 16th-century kitchen – the heart of the house

This is where THE LIFE is, with warmth from the great cooker which releases the intense perfumes of garlic, wines and herbs. Here is where the chopping and slicing and braising happens – where the bread rises and the jams bubble. Where we sit with our elbows on the table and talk about art and the meaning of poetry. Wine glows in the hand-blown glass and the food, often spicy with chillies, tastes of where it came from, and it is not the supermarket shelf.

Jams

My cupboard is full of jams – I try to make a very few pounds from each fruit as it comes into season. Rhubarb with angelica, apricot with its kernels, strawberries lightly cooked with lemon, raspberries, raspberries with plums, sweet orange, redpepper and lemon, chilli and apple jelly with chaenomeles. Somewhere there is gooseberry and elder, lots of damson, both jam and jelly, blackberry, elder, crab-applejelly and best of all quince – as cotignac, as conserve, as jelly and with vodka.

Marmalade

In January we start again with a coarse and bitter marmalade:

3 lbs of Sevilles
1 lb of lemons
3 lbs preserving sugar
approx - 2 pints water

Cut oranges and lemons in half. Gently cook with water until quite soft. I roughly cut two-thirds and squish the rest. Add preserving sugar – fast boil until set (test on a cold saucer) – it should take no more than twenty minutes. I never use more than 3/4 lb of sugar to each 1 lb of fruit with my jams – this should be enough for a set, without being too sweet. Many soft fruits have little pectin, so lemon juice is an essential addition. Quince has more pectin than any other fruit.

PRIVA

Char – potted fish

Since writing my original paper on char for the Oxford Symposium on Food and subsequently a shortened version for the Antique Collectors Club, I have come to appreciate more and more the virtue of this potted fish recipe. The dish itself has charm and is practical, and the recipe I now use is simple. Sadly char is not readily available, so I use organic brown trout.

1 large organic trout
6 oz butter salted
1 tsp mace
1 tsp black pepper
½ tsp cloves
1 tsp carraway seed

Pound the spices in the mortar. Place the dried trout in a buttered casserole. Sprinkle the spices inside and out. Cover with two-thirds of the butter and cook in a low oven for about 20 minutes (until the flesh leaves the bone). Remove skin and bone while still warm, then put the large flakes in your char pot, including all the spices, and cover with the melted butter. If the fish is not sufficiently smothered, melt the rest of the butter in the same pan and pour this over the fish.

It should be remembered that this is 16th-century food for keeping, so the taste is very strong. I have never met anyone who does not love this marvellously robust potted fish – it needs a correspondingly loud accompanying wine, maybe a Sauvignon.

Potted char in its lidded pot should keep in the fridge for at least a week. N.B. Dry the fish well as you do not want juices in this dish – they will limit its keeping powers. In the 16th century it would have lasted a month or so in the still room.

The char pot that I make, and keep in stock in my shop.

A Potter's Beans

At the moment I am enjoying making some large one-handled supper bowls that have a swan swimming in them. These bowls are for eating a 'mess of beans' in front of the open fire, particularly appropriate in our family as my daughter and her children live in a Tipi. When they are here, they do their same thing in the house, which is absolutely maddening – blackened pans and everyone naked on sheepskins by the ashy fire – but her cooking is superlative.

For the last fifty years I have had solid fuel cookers and latterly a huge magnificent oil-fired Stanley, and these and the open fire replicate, I'm sure, earlier ways of cooking, using both heavy pans and earthenware dishes. As I get older and seem to work even harder and longer hours in the pottery, and basically live on my own, the simpler the food the better, and the less time doing it also the better. I buy the best and freshest ingredients in season, and bake all my own bread with marvellous Loseley flour bought by the sack straight from the mill. Each baking is different from the last, with additions of rye, barley or white flour, with or without seeds or nuts and sometimes a wicked treat of pain brioche, gold with butter and eggs.

What a digression! Cooking beans – use beans of the day (dry), cover with water, two large garlic cloves, a branch of thyme and perhaps a few juniper berries, put in a cool oven at 6 p.m., adjust the water before bed, and next morning put in top oven. I scoop out some beans for pâté, salad or 'rissoles'. Have soup for lunch, shared with workers, and beans for supper. Next day there is the little bowl of beans in the fridge to make another meal.

My daughter Clio does this sort of thing on the open fire in a big black pot, often with layered contents (gipsy-like). Her food is extraordinary, from blackened chapatti to the wild weeds, funghi and mirabelle jam – all smoky and strongly flavoured.

The Quince (*Cydonia oblonga*)

Cyril Connolly, the essayist, wrote in *The Unquiet Grave*: 'there are artists like quinces – *des vrais coings*: their fragrance doth not cloy.'

The quince is a taut, heavy-hipped fruit in a vivid daffodil jacket and no mood to be eaten without exertion. To many people the quince has scant appeal. 'What', they ask, 'do you do with it?' Connolly chose that fruit as an emblem of civilisation in Europe, with its hard, tough flesh, bright colour and unearthly savour. The quince, like the pomegranate and the fig, is an antique symbol of love, passion and fecundity common to numerous cultures. In Eastern Daghestan, wild quinces may be observed in great numbers, and in the autumn when the fruit is ripening, the traveller passing through might think himself in the Gardens of Paradise. Despite its hot country origins, the English quince endured and during the 16th century, it was mentioned by all the authors of books on fruit culture. There is an account in 1275 of four quince trees planted in the Royal Gardens of the Tower of London. The seeds were taken by English settlers to many countries, including Argentina, Australia, Brazil, Canada, America and Poland.

The name comes from the old French *coign*, leading at last to quince. Parkinson, writing in the 17th century, gushed that 'there is no fruit growing in the land that has so many excellent uses'. Quinces were baked whole with sugar and butter and baked, sliced or puréed with and without apples into puddings and pies, as well as the spiced English sweetmeat Chare de Quyinces, also called continiate or quince confort.

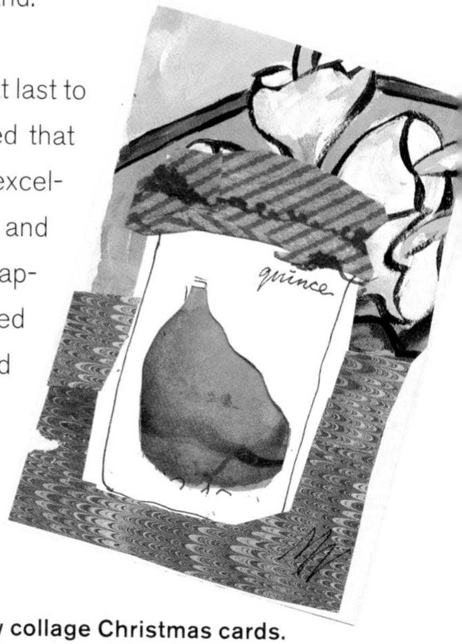

The cultivation of the tree has waned, but as can be seen from the photographs it is well worth planting

Opposite: The exquisite quince blossom; right: one of my collage Christmas cards.

now for the beauty of its blossom and the fragrance and function of its fruit. The variety I grow is Portugal. This was imported to England from Holland by the older John Tradescant, gardener to the Earl of Salisbury, in 1611. This type has been deemed less harsh and more tender and juicy than its rivals and is of the highest quality. Although Meech and Champion varieties may produce more fruit, they are not notable for flavour. Portugal is almost more of a bush than a tree and, if heavily pruned each year, one can keep it to a comfortable size and shape, which also seems to encourage the production of fruit.

Quince Conserves

We start by making jelly with about 3 lbs of roughly cut whole ripe quince in maybe 3 pints of water. Cook slowly until soft – place all this in muslin and let it drip overnight. Use 1 pint of the quince liquid to 3/4 lbs of sugar. Cook fast – it will set very quickly and become a perfect rose colour. It is the most exotic and beautiful of all preserves.

Quince Cotignac

Weigh the quince pulp (which contains pips, cores and skin). Squish or blend to a kind of coarse purée. Add 3/4 lb of sugar to each 1 lb of pulp and cook carefully – it will glop and glook and hiss. Do not burn. When it sets, pour into Swiss Roll tins lined with greaseproof paper and dry in a cool oven. Cut into squares and pack into jars, tins or boxes surrounded with caster sugar.

Each year a pot of cotignac is given as a small Christmas present to friends. As a sweetmeat it can be eaten with cheese or taken with coffee at the end of a meal. In the South of France, it is known as pâté de coing and in Spain as membrillo.

Quince Conserve

1 lb quince, 3/4 lb sugar, approximately 1 pint water

This is time-consuming, as we are paring and coring the fruit and cutting it into neat, small chunks.

Cook fruit slowly until soft. Add the sugar – brisk boil – test for set. This should be quite soon, about fifteen minutes. It is a beautiful rose colour, but the taste is not quite as marvellous as the reduced jelly. The jars should be very clean and warm. I use the cellophane jam-jar tops as well as screw tops. Pot just off the boil.

This year we had a good harvest, and these golden fruits fill the house with their perfume and contain the promise of the wonderful conserves and drink I shall make from them. The little trug is Edwardian.

Previous pages: the quince tree in full bloom.
Left and above: quinces have had a huge influence on my work as a potter, particularly in the last ten years, as you can see from the work shown here.

The medlar (*Mespilus germanica*)

The medlar is a small or middle-sized branching tree and is a native of Southern Europe. J.C. Loudon (1822) states that it is naturalised in parts of England where it has been sown in copse. It can be propagated by seeds, layers or cuttings. Millar says if the ripe seeds are planted immediately, they will come up the next spring and make good plants in two years.

It is strange that Loudon does not mention the edibility of the fruit or its remarkable form. The French describe this as *col de poule*. Sir William Robinson, writing in 1911, describes it as a beautiful small tree with large and handsome flowers, and suggests it is a perfect lawn tree, flowering around the middle of May. He also makes no mention of the fruit.

According to Professor Malins, the great pruning expert, the medlar comes from Asia Minor and Europe. He describes the fruit as being 'wide and brown and apple shaped, with an open eye, surrounded by the persistent calyx. The fruits to be left on the tree until leaf fall, then stored until "bletted".'

This small tree is charming in its standard form and I keep it in a nice 'umbrella' shape by ruthlessly removing all the new upright growth as it appears. The single white flowers with their prevalent stamens arise from a corolla of large, pale-ish leaves and are charming. The fruit with its rather bum-like appearance is intriguing, and I love the taste – but it is acquired, unusual and somehow from another epoch; I fancy Tudor.

Here is the recipe for the excellent jam. Jane Grigson mentions that it can be made into 'a sort of liqueur with syrup and brandy'. I have not tried this, but prefer the idea of making a drink with vodka, as I do with the quince.

To sum up – it is a charming small tree, full of interest and, like so many things in my garden, parts of it are edible.

Opposite: the blossom, the fruit and my painting of the medlar tree.

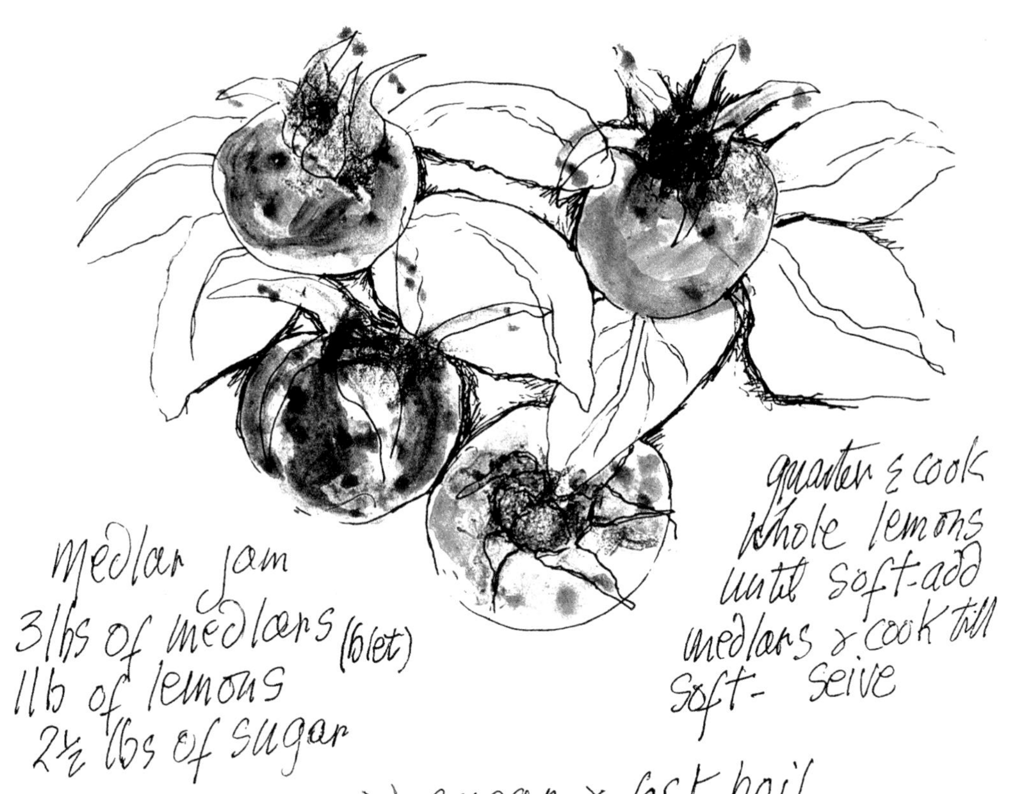

medlar jam
3lbs of medlars (blet)
1lb of lemons
2½ lbs of sugar

quarter & cook
whole lemons
until soft - add
medlars & cook till
soft - seive

add sugar & fast boil
until setting
this is good with meat or cheese
as well as with scones -
the taste is somewhat between prunes
and chesnuts

In the early spring, I am out with my basket picking the wild greens – all when the leaves are small. Hogweed, ground elder, dead nettle, nettle, sorrel, wild garlic (ramsons), dock and dandelion. Rinse and cook for about eight minutes then serve with lots of butter and black pepper. The taste is strong, even intense, and must be similar to the *herbes* gathered by the peasants in the 16th century

In the autumn I wander off into the woods to collect mushrooms.
Shown here are :
1. the morel which appeared in the herb garden
2. wood blewetts
3. chanterelles
4. sliced boletus drying for the winter
5. a plate of russullas and boletus
6. beautiful but inedible funghi

5
4

Above: Wild mushrooms, gathered from the woods and commons each autumn, are an important part of my very seasonal life. They are both beautiful and edible, and also inspirational as decorative subjects for pots and paintings. Opposite pictures: The cardoons that I raised from seed are very hardy and magnificent to look at. Although they seem to be a speciality in France and Italy, I have never succeeded in cooking the stems satisfactorily – despite three blanchings they still remain bitter and taste unpleasant. In the photograph below left they are coming into flower, and below right are the small purple artichokes from Rome.

a cardoon
Not an
artichoke
it grows to
the stems
are
edible
But I have
3 times
then
with
butter
the result
was
BITTER
THIS

the garden

A place to walk on narrow green paths, a place to sit and share good food and a place for foolish sculptures and foolish fountains

Above and opposite: As with most of my furniture, I found this curly metal chair in a junk shop. It inspired this woodcut, opposite, by my friend Anne Hayward, which is the first in a charming series set in the garden and reproduced in this book. How I admire the skill and intricate detail of her work. Augusta landed up under the old potato basket full of young lettuce plants.

'Mary's dream garden – Summer chair.' Anne Hayward

Top: My bedroom window and bay tree, south facing. Above left: The 16th-century kitchen window from the garden, and beside it the lavatory window. Right: The garden shed. Opposite: This was once a privy, then a bantam shed, and now I keep some tools here.

Making a garden – wild and tranquil spaces

The garden is an extension of my house. It has different rooms; not in the superb Sissinghurst sense – hedge-bounded – but with places to sit and to see blue tits and bumble bees.

Everywhere the tall hogweed hosts a hundred insects, which the small birds chase. Lunching under the old rose arbour we watch butterflies emerging from the damson hedge and stinging nettles.

There is a spot where the early morning sun catches chandelier lustres which hang from an old galvanized basket. Here I have my breakfast.

The raised herb garden is formal with hand-made bricks from Selborne. Its pink sequestered floor is punctuated with thrown pots planted with thymes, savory and angelica.

Surprisingly my garden is tranquil despite the recent 'assemblages' – crazy fountains made

The fecund rose 'New Dawn' scrambles wildly over the ancient tiled roof and leaded window of my bathroom in the upper storey of the oldest part of the house.
It is often difficult to open the window; indeed in the summer I like to keep it open so the roses droop over the wash basin.
Above: Anne Hayward's wood engraving of my early 20th-century *bruette* (wheelbarrow).

from found objects, galvanized baths and cans, painted sinks and old lawn mowers.

Every part of the place nurtures something unusual, from cardoons and sea-kale to the ruins of a 17th-century elm.

Nothing is as you expect; one must search for the rare trees and hedge plants. Best of all are the precious quince tree hung about with yellow velvet fruit and the medlar with its strange bunched 'brown' growth, which the French call 'chicken's arse'.

In the pottery garden a 1930s beehive surmounts a herb mound, with outsize ceramic bees crouching above it, and groups of beautiful terracotta pots are entwined with ivies.

A speckled giraffe twenty feet tall rises above a tiny meadow thick with corn cockle, poppies, yellow rattle and fritillaries (see page 94).

Previous page (78): the north side of the house in the early morning, looking towards the drawing room.
Previous page (79), clockwise from top left: The arbour with the inverted rhubarb pot on a chimney; the pottery garden path with dandelions and forget-me-nots; the Great Spanish pot in spring; the same pot in summer, seen from the house in the photo opposite.
These pages: In the snow the chandelier is nearer to Anne Hayward's tender wood engraving, and everything takes on a new dimension, reminding me how much Nature exceeds ART and how humble we must remain before that which is our inspiration.

These batter'd tools rest against the broken wall near my basket chandelier (see also page 81, and above). Everything is seen in relation to something else – nothing is isolated. These bricks were made here at least a hundred years ago by Surrey craftsmen.

Previous page (85), clockwise from top left: Japanese anemone against the north-facing house wall; Hostas and Welsh poppies; the old lavatory pan with a pottery owl; Nicotiana in the great 19 th-century pot. Page 86: The Bramley overburden'd in May, with my Edwardian apple ladder. Opposite: The great wagon is returning to the earth from whence it came – as is the milk float and the farm tip, above and left. When the children were small we all had a cart each and slept outside in them during the summer. We dined with our friends in the larger one.

The Herb Garden

I have always had herb gardens but in 1993, the year of my 70th birthday, I received a small bequest and decided to design a more structured space. Previously the strong plants had grown out of control, with elecampane, rosemary and sage completely overshadowing everything except the bloody lemon balm.

Mr Voller, a master bricklayer, was recommended to me, and I ordered hand-made bricks and paviors from Selborne. Joy Jardine and I plotted and measured out the area which I wanted to be, as it were, a room with raised beds of different heights over a zig-zag floor. Mr Voller did this very skilfully over a period of about four weeks. The bricks were laid on sand and we turfed the surrounding area on completion. This was all built on the site of the previous herb garden. All the good plants were dug into the vegetable garden to await their new home. We had to have two loads of top soil with plenty of broken brick beneath. Then, the tiring job of replanting began in the early spring. To my surprise this was very successful even in its first year, as can be seen in the photo, opposite below.

At the time of that project I did not realise that my arthritis would make me very lame, and now these raised beds are not only aesthetically pleasing but truly functional. This ten-year-old brick herb garden (seen recently below right and opposite, above) with its 'fan' design continues to be a joy.

My children Clio, Claudia and Hugo commissioned three large pots, decorated with my monogram, from that great potter Mick Pinner, and they still look splendid planted with thymes and bergamot. In the overall design there is a sunken circle of bricks which is always graced with angelica.

'Mary's dream garden - Beneath the pear tree.' Anne Hayward

Above: Anne Hayward's evocative wood engraving of the heavily pruned 'weeping' pear. Right: a photograph of the same subject.

Above: The 'hay flower' fashioned from an old rick cutter, a *kugelhopf* mould and a cake tray. Chris Lovell made the copper cat. Left: *chaise percée* with objects.
Overleaf, clockwise from top left:
The snail; the lavatory seat rostrum; old flower pots in an urn; ruins of the ancient elm and a French saloir from Gers; this Winchconme kiln waster is where the great tit nests (the leaves are the dreaded giant hogweed); the tractor tyre monster; French dove cage; badger's skull found when wild mushroom gathering.

Opposite and above: A speckled giraffe twenty feet tall rises above a tiny meadow thick with corn cockle, poppies, yellow rattle and fritillaries. This was made when the telephone engineers put in a new pole. They sawed this one into three for me. The head was once Hugo's cut-out monkey, the body a chair seat; the baby has a bit of dressing-table for the face and an old birch broom for the tail. By the giraffe is the truncated Balsam poplar sucker. My daughter Clio has woven prunings from the crab apple, willow and a blue plastic sack around it.

Above and opposite: The blue trellis, hung about with silly objects and pieces of plastic tablecloth, makes a gateway to the rough garden, compost heap and clothes line. My grandson Nuku and I are making a funny ladder to a fruit tree.

Water – wacky fountains made from found objects

The fountains began in their funny way when I found myself unable to make a satisfactory ceramic one. The complexities of the water rise, hiding the pump, trailing the electric flex from A to B and then of course the fall – the rise and fall have to be equal. I had a pile of old watering cans, baths, bird-feeders lying around in various stages of dilapidation, and a pair of long taps and some old hose were helpful. The first pump cost £35, but the water rise was only eighteen inches, and hours were spent fiddling about until it sort of worked. Then the wind blows or a blackbird lands on a tap. This fountain was built in the pottery garden.

Then I wanted one to watch while I ate my lunch in the conservatory, so two sinks were heaved into place and each year different objects were put around the rim, the water coloured blue. The result was extremely entertaining. Sadly within ten days the wicked algae arrived and everything needed cleaning. The best fountain turned out to be the one with the mermaids and glasses and crystal drops (see page 104).

I found an urinal in the antique centre, rested it on a night-soil bucket and filled it with colourless marbles. Some transparent hose carried the water to the top – simple and successful.

The fourth one was a bit fiddly. The container was an Atco grass collector with some funnels to hide the pump, an iron graveyard vase to receive the water which, in its turn, hit a ping-pong ball. We floated plastic vegetables on the surface. Everything keeps slipping and sliding, but it is next to my breakfast and supper table. I like to hear the gentle plash of the water.

Of course it is all fun and much admired, but such a time waster.

Previous page and left: Galvanized fountain 2004. We have a different one each year but this is the best so far.
Pages 102–5 overleaf: the development of the sink fountains.

Above: The Badoit sink fountain, around 2002. Opposite, both pictures: The tuneful one made from a saloir and a copper pub funnel.

Opposite:The Atco and funnel fountain, and, below, an earlier effort with 1920s cemetery 'vases' and plastic zinnia.
Above: The complex, 2002, nearly all enamel *folie*.

the camera's eye

Maybe this is the Artist's eye – capturing the early morning light as it slants across the kitchen table, enlivens the lace curtains or lingers for a second on a dew-soaked spider's web

Opposite: A mad lace curtain
in the downstairs lavatory.
Overleaf: the kitchen window.

Lace curtains – memories of France

It was not until 1985, when researching slipware in Hungary, that I bought my first SLR camera. I manage to take some serious pictures but never use flash. When the very early morning sun streaks through the east window I grab my camera and try to capture the light that illumines the overburdened kitchen table.

I love the mysterious light that lingers on these old French curtains (right). When I am in the markets or the *brocantes* in Brittany I search for them, and find in them an evocation of the 19th-century French Impressionist paintings which gives to my 16th-century English cottage, along with the red-checked plastic table cloth, a Continental feel.

In 1990, my journey to the Auvergne was enhanced, as are all French journeys, by the very otherness of the houses we drove past. By the shutter-framed windows and the cascades of small-flowered geraniums. These windows were shut, and instead of their usual blank stares, wild white scenes were framed between the shutters – lace curtains within curtains, draped and looped, defining strange pictures: Mount Fujiyama hovering over a small lake, swans swimming beyond a vase of flowers and a hundred other designs.

Where can such ridiculous things be bought? Even in this unexplored part of France I have been unable to find any old-fashioned shops, or rather, there are old-fashioned shops selling new-fashioned things. Fortunately for me, Thursday is market day in Langeac. Every street and square is crowded with stalls (including the local taxidermist).

I love the mysterious light that both lingers on and pierces these old French curtains and makes my glass drops sparkle. They send wild prisms all over the kitchen at different times of the day – I take my camera and record that chance moment.

Between the cheese producers and the vegetable stalls sits a large estate car draped with lace curtains, and alongside the River Allier are trestle tables covered in rolls of lace. There anyone can buy a dream – castles on the Rhine, 18th-century maidens on a swing, or cats sitting by the glowing fire.

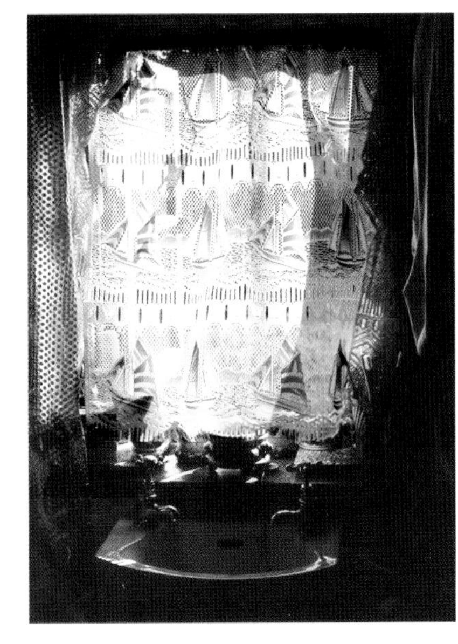

In all my daily explorations I only found one old-fashioned *mercerie* and that was in Billom, about twenty kilometres from Issoire. Mattress ticking was stacked on the shelves. There were dark, small-patterned cottons for *tabliers*, check napkins, thick lace curtains, striped canvas for deck chairs and every kind of gingham for tablecloths as well as curtain tie-backs and tassels. Net curtains of all types were for sale by the metre but, inevitably, it was 11.45 a.m. I did ultimately buy two 'pairs' of curtains from a market stall and these now grace my own and the spare bedroom. Visitors are sharply divided into those who love them and those who hate them. The curtains are not antique, not chic, but FUN.

Opposite and above and left: My downstairs bathroom is painted in glorious blue and yellow, as shown in my painting opposite. The coloured lace curtain with its little boats is one of my favourites, creating fascinating patterns on the wall when the sun shines. These I bought by the metre in a Breton market. On the right of the picture is a pair of 18th-century cotton stockings. This room was previously a lavatory and cupboard. Now it also contains a beneficial shower as I can seldom climb the stairs to the old bathroom.

Above: I am not particularly keen on cutting flowers and bringing them into the house, but on this occasion I broke the rules. It must be 7 o'clock in the morning and this unsubtle rose, 'New Dawn', reminds me of a Fantin Latour painting.

Opposite: On another day I put the poppies by the blue glass. They arrive in the vegetable plot and each morning I pick a new bunch. The kitchen jars date from the 1930s and belonged to my mother.

I have always been an early riser and I often can't resist rushing outside when those first few rays of sun break through the trees. You can see I found the dew and managed to fetch my camera before the magic melted away.

A large fishy honey-glazed dish which I made in 2002.

the work

I opened my first pottery workshop and shop thirty years ago in Godalming High Street, and only moved it to Brickfields in 1984

TÄRA·LITT

Here I am on the wheel decorating a nine-inch commemorative plate with the famous slip trailer that I designed from bicycle inner-tubes, wine corks and a pipette and bulldog clip. In the 17th century they would have used a cow horn and goose quill. The plate is decorated whilst still wet and attached to the throwing bat.

A workshop of my own – how it all started

My interest in pottery was first aroused after taking local evening classes at Farnham College of Art. After that I made the big leap and opened my first workshop and shop in Godalming. Eventually I was able to buy the derelict stables. With help from COSIRA the barn became my new larger workshop and what had been the garage became my little shop.

A potter's day

It is nine o'clock and Tibs is scratching at the door. Of course I have been up since seven checking the kiln, and there is a deep pink sky reflected in the flooded field. I rush for the camera. There are two shots left and, as I try to focus, a flotilla of ducks emerges from behind the hedge. It is beautiful and so different from three weeks ago when I discovered the office, workshops and shop under four inches of water. The clay store and sheds were also immersed. Well, now

Left: this photo was taken in 1968 at Farnham College of Art, where I learnt to pot one day a week with these marvellous women who both endured and helped me over a period of four years. I am third from left.

Opposite below: the interior of the workshop showing the two Cromartie kilns and the big bins of glaze. Opposite above: me working on the 3D self portrait made from many thrown elements. It is about twelve inches high.

that is all cleared up and every doorway has a sandbag barricade which I dare not move.

Fortunately Heather comes today and will clear up my mess in the house and make it look beautiful. We discuss the priorities – logs for the fire and hoovering the cushions (cat hairs) – as people are coming to dinner. Now Angela is here to fill the trailers and organise the pottery mess. I slip a charger, a gift for the wife who is doing an MA on fossils. Lots of references, piccie of Mary Anning who in 1860 discovered the first plesiosaur in Lyme Regis. I trail the marvellous bones – not bad. We have to prepare a bisque, putting the biggest dishes on the floor at the back of the kiln. For some reason if they are on the front shelves, near the door, they break. The telephone rings: some poor sod wants to sell me financial advice. I give him some. A nice customer has come to collect two small birthday bowls. I have put 5 April instead of May. Profuse apologies and will have to remake. Fortunately they are only 400 grams of clay and fit round larger plates in the kiln. An interesting parcel arrives. It is the photo-scan of my new book which must be proofread within the next ten days. As I do not have even a washing machine, let alone a computer, this involves a great deal of writing, dictating and agonising with my long-suffering secretary.

We always have a serious lunch break. There will be a good soup, salad and bread and cheese. There is absolutely no time to agonise about health issues. My excessively high blood pressure is, I believe, the driving force, and my arthritis gives me the opportunity to sport a handsome ebony cane embellished with silver.

Sadly now, I have to throw a charger – with only six kilos of clay. I can't manage more weight and tomorrow I shall fill the trailers and face up to decorating it. Well, this great oeuvre is going to be Punchinello and Toby and 'That's the way to do it' repeated around the rim. At this stage it will be handsome, but my erratic turning, the kiln and the atmosphere will ultimately translate this good piece of work into a load of shit I suspect.

Now it is time for Angela to leave and I must deal with the clay she has prepared for the day's throwing. The phone rings and it is Emmanuel Cooper asking me to write 'a day in the life of a potter'. It is five o'clock and I still have another five pieces to throw for my larger unicorn, a three dimensional object to keep my lion company. Tibs says it is tea-time and at last I crawl into the shower before lighting the fire and groping for the Calvados, totally forgetting people are coming at seven. Another Calvados, intensely creative cookery, a car arrives and we sit down to marvellous food and wine and talk, discussing the role of the potter in society. We eat smoked trout pâté I made yesterday, followed by a gougère with spinach and tomatoes provençales. A perfect camembert and salad and those white Italian Muscat grapes that are now in season. We drink a Saumur and an excellent Chilean Merlot. No one stays late as we all work tomorrow, and I stagger to bed ticking off in my head all those jobs I had to do and have, yes, done.

As you get older sleep is elusive and today (it is my eightieth) I am a year older. Must set the alarm as I have to assemble the unicorn tomorrow before it gets too dry. The kiln has fired overnight and there is a photographer coming tomorrow to collect some pots. This is a fairly typical day.

Opposite: the flooded field at dawn. Above: the exterior of my little shop (formerly the garage); left: the wet, newly decorated plate on the wheelhead.

I adore the work of Chardin and made these drawings from the useful pots I saw in his painting; Proust is another hero.

hevées - où il n'y a pas une seule touche
ù chaque partie reçoit des autres
d'être comme elle leur
'a sienne"

Proust

Chardin

MV

What is slipware ?

What is meant by slipware? It sounds like skating or sliding, not like pottery, and many people seem to be unclear about the meaning of this term.

Firstly, it is lead-glazed earthenware – firing temperature between 890 and 1100 degrees centigrade. Secondly, the pots are decorated with coloured slip before they are fired in the kiln. Slip is clay mixed with water. If it is used for covering the body of the pot, then I call it pouring slip, or engobe. It has a thin, batter-like consistency, and is usually of a contrasting colour to the body clay; for example, white on a red clay.

Slip trailing is the method of decorating the pot with slip from either a cow-horn, a small clay vessel and quill, rubber bulb and pipette, or the 'Mary Wondrausch inner tube and pipette'. For this last technique, thicker slip is used and lightly extruded.

All work that is earthenware and decorated in any way with slips before firing is called slipware. This includes sgraffito, which is the technique of scratching through a leather-hard covering slip to reveal the contrasting clay body underneath, or in some cases to reveal another slip applied below, as in Beauvais ware.

There is an additional group of wares that come roughly under the sgraffito heading as the possibilities of the method are explored. For example: brushing different coloured slips on to the leather-hard background; cutting out the background to reveal large areas of body colour; painting with oxides such as copper and cobalt to enhance

Opposite above: 'pearling'. Below: my Millennium cup.
Right: 'Queenie'. We only made fifty-two of
these – a sort of limited edition.

the scratched drawing. A combination of all these techniques can be used together on the same pot. Other decorative techniques normally associated with slipware are marbling and feathering.

Slip-decorated earthenware is not to be confused with majolica (or Faience or Delftware), where the painting is applied on top of a tin glaze after the first firing. The common feature of majolica and slipware is that they are both earthenware.

From earliest times, painted slips were used as decoration. The most familiar of these pots come from China, Ancient Greece, Byzantium, Egypt, Italy and also from Britain during the period of Roman domination, when the Castor wares from Northamptonshire were made and decorated as they were in Germany at this time.

Lead-glazed, slip-coated wares were imported to Britain from Beauvais and Saintes in France in the 14th century, and are found in quantity in many excavated sites. Literally hundreds of chafing dishes (coal pots) from Saintes, know as Saintonge wares, have been excavated all over Britain, undecorated except for splashes of glaze. La Chapelle des Pots near Saintes was known for its strange barrel-type wine containers, heavily embossed and lead-glazed. Slipware was made here until the beginning of the 20th century. Now in the 1980s there is a large factory on the same site, producing jigger and jolleyed and moulded imitation Renaissance and 18th-century Faience!

Left and opposite: Two three-dimensional figures twelve inches high – the Lion and the Unicorn, inspired by the 17th-century Thomas Toft charger. They are constructed from many wheel-thrown pieces and each black line is pearled in the Toft manner. They are slip-trailed under a dark honey glaze. The proud Lion is in the Victoria and Albert Museum, London.

Below and opposite: All these pieces of mine are trailed in the traditional manner. The inspiration comes from English 17th-century wares. There is also a strong Continental influence, which you can see in the jug shapes.

The future of skill

I have been thinking a great deal about the role of the potter in 21st-century society, where technology prevails. One looks at much of the work of graduates and potters and sees how the camera in one form or another dominates the medium, and how little functional work is produced.

Times have changed, and that wonderful image of the studio potter making soup bowls and spice containers for the discriminating buyer has almost certainly disappeared. There are very few good galleries that sell pottery, but many that sell ceramic art works. In the 1940s, 1950s and 1960s, Primavera, a wonderful shop in Sloane Street, Chelsea, owned by Henry Rothschild, sold useful pots by David Eels, David Leach and others. Living and working just down the road, I passed (and entered) this shop daily, with no idea that some twenty-five years later I too would become a potter, making cornflake bowls for my children and subsequently for sale to a wider audience.

At one time I was a cook and later ran a small cookery school, and now I write about the history of food, which means that the exact use of a pot has been of paramount interest to me for some sixty years. Travelling around Europe, visiting local museums and the markets, staying with old country people and asking them about their diet, their potagères, their marine culture etc., has absorbed what little 'free' time I have. Although I sometimes use a camera, mainly I draw and measure old pots that I discover.

BLESSINGS ON FIONA AND ANATOLE
GEORGE + MARGARE
GOLDEN WEDDING

These cheese platters of mine are all made using a technique known as sgraffito, where the image is scratched through a coloured slip to reveal the contrasting body below. I mastered this art when I wanted to make a change from the slipware I was becoming well known for. I take most of my inspiration for the designs from the goings-on in my kitchen. I always keep a good selection of platters in my shop, and there are always salt kits, owl jugs, punch bowls, char pots, salad bowls and egg stands.

Above: Just some of the everyday useful pots I made, inspired by Hungarian themes.
Left: A large fish dish, sgraffito, brushed slip and painted oxides under a clear glaze.

Examples of my 21st-century work. Opposite is one of my preparatory drawings for the fig plates shown above: the one in front includes quinces as well as figs. These pieces are sgraffito, nine-inch diameter, and painted with blue and orange slip under a clear glaze. The reverse is also decorated and the rim is pierced for hanging.

In the move from the open fire to the iron range, the base of cooking pots has been entirely changed from a rounded to a large flat form. Enamel, aluminium, stainless steel and now, once again, cast-iron forms have followed. There is still a place for well-thrown earthenware pieces – gratin dishes and casseroles – which the French and Spanish make wonderfully well, as do a few of our English potters, but the movement away from functional pottery towards sculptural and 'artistic' forms is the modality. In my rural workshop, the impression that I receive is that the Crafts Council prefers to see pots as Art Works and I am amused when asked to enter the number of 'works' on an exhibition list, rather than the number of pots.

To make a pot, we must have skills – truly basic skills – firstly making the clay usable by pugging, wedging, kneading, weighing and balling, then throwing the pot on the wheel, followed by the dreaded turning of the perfect foot rim, the pulling of a strong handle on the pot and, last of all and the most difficult, decorating the vessel in an appropriate way. Allied to these formal skills is the paramount understanding of what we use and what we use it for, how relevant this is to our customers and, subsequently, if we can persuade (educate) them that this is what they themselves need as opposed to buying a Christmas or birthday present. Apart from all these reasonably simple tasks, the potter fulfils what I believe to be a fundamental role in the community, in being, perhaps, the only relic of a magical time past – the simple craftsman in a village deprived of blacksmiths, cobblers, saddlers and carpenters. I do not mean 'the good old days' in a romantic sense, but a time where people were in touch with where things came from. Milk from the udder, wheat from the field, peas in the pod. It is no joke that the girl on the check-out does not recognise a broad bean but rings up a persimmon. As working potters, we are the link to the earth. We are the monstrous relics of a marvellous time when designs and ideas flew from men, as opposed to machines. A time when craft was a noble word.

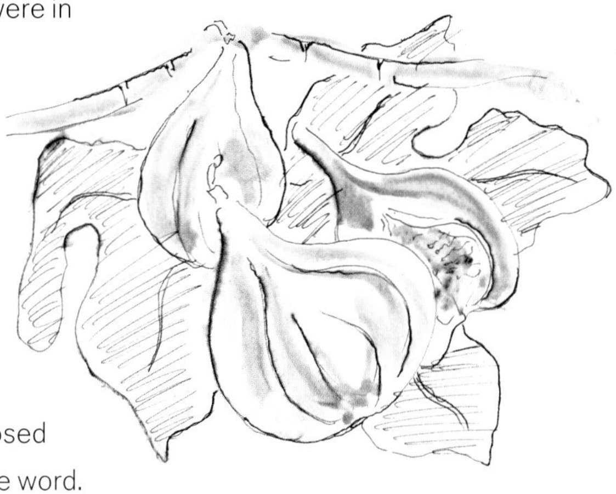

Some of the Christmas cards that I make & paint each year.

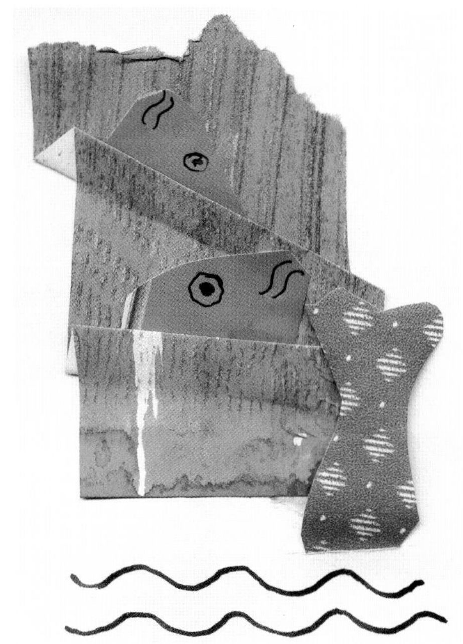

Acknowledgements

Special thanks to Mike Tighe for the design
Joy Hulen & Sue Matthews for the typing
to Heather for keeping my house in good order
Paul et Jeonie for working the garden
And, of course Angela for all
her work in the pottery over 20 years

MW

Thank you to the following for allowing me to use their photographs in this book:
James Merrell/Country Living Magazine pages 24, 42 & 53(top), Andreas von Einsiedel/BBC Good Food 26,
Christopher Simon Sykes /Interior Archive 28/29, 40, 48, 49, Liese Siegelman/The World of Interiors
magazine 34/35, Michael Tighe 72, 74, 75, 93(below), & 96(below right), Jason Lane 94, Laurence Bulaitis 124.
All the other photographs in this book are my own.

First published in 2004 by Mary Wondrausch OBE
Brickfields, Compton, Surrey, Gu13 1HZ

ISBN 0-9548237-0-2

Printed and bound by Cromwell Press, Trowbridge, UK